T0157331

DANCE of the HEART

DANCE of the HEART

Grace VanSciver

ARCHWAY
PUBLISHING

Archway Publishing books may be ordered through booksellers or by contacting:

Archway Publishing
1663 Liberty Drive
Bloomington, IN 47403
www.archwaypublishing.com
1 (888) 242-5904

Interior Image Credit: Amanda Byler Photography

ISBN: 978-1-4808-8095-5 (sc)
ISBN: 978-1-4808-8096-2 (hc)
ISBN: 978-1-4808-8094-8 (e)

Library of Congress Control Number: 2019912968

Print information available on the last page.

Archway Publishing rev. date: 9/18/2019

For my family and friends who have allowed my heart to dance.

The
HEART

We hate the things we can't control, but we need what they bring us, so we yell at the rain but long for the strawberries.

I think we're all brave, the way we keep on going despite knowing that, ultimately, we're not in control.

The glittering surface we are so attracted to would quickly lose its luster if we could see what carefully hidden darkness lurks inside the soul.

I'm lost in a mirage of you, never sure which version of you is real or which is my own lovesick illusion.

There's something magical about finding a person with whom your soul connects, almost as magical as finding a constellation in the night sky.

Be brave enough to let your heart fall in love with new things, new people.

Is there ever really silence? Because all I hear in the quiet is my soul speaking endlessly of you.

Her greatest attribute? I'd have to say the way she so easily found meaning in what others deemed meaningless.

It wasn't death that was so painful; they would always have the memories of yesterday. It was the loss of shared tomorrows that was unsettling. It was the realization of a shortened forever.

Their love was like a loaded gun. Their lies formed a daring finger around the trigger, leaving only a future of deadly explosion.

The worst kind of bondage is the bondage of the soul.

It was too late for him to turn around, for he had already fallen in love with the enigma that she presented.

They say home is where the heart is, and it's no secret well-kept that my heart is with you. I was fearful, and while it's no excuse, lashing out in anger was my response to the realization that I would be without you. And that was something that I found impossible for my heart to take. But after further pondering, I realized that the sheer fact that my miniscule dot on the timeline overlapped with yours is a miracle. I am lucky, even if it all was just for a little while, because some go their whole lives as temporary tenants, never finding a true place of safety and comfort. But I experienced the ultimate luxury anyone really has who is lucky enough to find someone like you. Something like we have, a place for our hearts to call home.

"Why can't we at least know when they'll leave us?" wept the widow.

"Because," answered her friend, "we'd live our lives as one moment lost rather than one moment gained."

"If you could have any supernatural ability for one day, what would it be?" he asked.

"The ability to read hearts," she somberly replied.

"Why?"

"To see if you really still love me at my worst."

The haze, laid upon her by his gaze, left her trapped in a lovesick daze.

We all wonder why our souls feel so heavy. We complain of their incompetence as we're forced to endure depression, anxiety, and that seemingly ever-present cloud of self-doubt. Yet unknowingly, we burden our souls ourselves with all the secrets we subconsciously force them to bear.

We're told from birth that nothing is forever. So why are we so sure that love will be?

"There are plenty of other fish in the sea," they say, almost robotically, as if finding someone new will erase the memory of another. They just don't understand that against my better judgement, my heart's only searching for one.

If given a non-refillable bottle of love, would you drink it right away or save it only to drink in increments on the days you need it most?

The memories of us loom like a silhouette in the shadows of my past.

Embrace the spirit of younger you.

You're my guide in the fog of it all. An ever-steady constant when the road ahead is unclear simply in the way you shine so brightly.

They told them they wouldn't be compatible. "Too different" was their excuse. But isn't a sock just as effective, whether or not the pair is identical?

Self-love comes after you've learned to value the exclusive gifts you uniquely have to offer the world.

She made him into a him he was proud of.

The best thing you can do for people is to hear them in whatever way they choose to speak.

You can love the human being and disagree with the conversation.

The worst way to love is to love when they're gone.

Her heart burned as the lines blurred between loving when she felt she shouldn't and not loving when she felt she should.

"How do I know I can trust you?" he asked.

"Honesty is hard to come by," she replied, "and I want to be one of the rare ones."

I let my pride get in the way. I really wanted you to stay.

The heart is a resource most hesitant to follow because of the ever-looming question: will it ever lie?

Looking in the mirror, I didn't see myself at first. Instead, I saw everything and everyone that made tomorrow an exciting challenge to conquer. And then the realization hit; I finally found myself. It wasn't really a "new me," but the new ability to willingly accept everything and everyone that made me *me*. And when the haze on the mirror finally faded away, I saw myself. I was smiling, and it was no longer fake.

To genuinely love someone without first loving yourself is as impossible a task as attempting to tame the wind.

Presuming was she. Too sure of herself to hide behind games and riddles, unafraid to meet the uncut truth head-on and dare it to try and hurt her.

They were just foolish, getting matching ink before knowing the definition of permanent.

Time doesn't shorten our days with the ones we love; our lack of attention to it does.

I haven't quite decided if it's the brave or the foolish who experiment with fate.

The way I see it, what you define as "mine" will never fully be yours. I think I learned to love myself when I realized the only thing I truly have full ownership of is me.

She didn't have a man. She didn't need someone to affirm what she already knew: her worth.

They tried to label temporary infatuation as "love," which ended as catastrophically as mistaking TNT for a candle.

Here's to the souls as indecisive as mine.

She looked about the room from the vantage point of the corner, afraid to talk to anyone for fear that they too would scar her with the knife of betrayal.

I say *bored* is the worst state for a heart to be, as you're left endlessly searching for something to entertain it again.

I realize now that bad things can have a positive outcome. See, while I'm in love with you, I realize you could never love me back. And now, knowing you're hurting breaks me more than you not loving me ever could. I've finally learned that true love sometimes means letting go.

The pair was caught in a cosmic bubble. The speckled sky was closer than it's ever been as they danced on the rooftop to the music of the city.

Their love was like a hot summer's evening breeze ... calm, refreshing, and unexpected.

When the wrinkles blanket her face and the days are spent on the wood of a rocking chair, passing the time with crossword puzzles and black coffee, love her. For loving when the beauties of youth are gone proves love is deeper than circumstance or appearances. It's when those still living in their youth will watch you and be left in awe of love.

Does loving yourself come surrounded by people affirming your worth or walking in some Christmas-laden boulevard alone and content because you're finally at peace?

It was then I realized it wasn't they who made her fearful but a misinterpreted reflection of herself.

She was tired of heartlessly continuing through the rote routine of it all.

He looked at sunsets like he looked at the world: beautifully designed just for him.

I'm in love with the city, which is a terrible reality because my heart is bored if I'm anywhere but there. And bored is a terrible state for a heart to be.

Love can be a dangerous thing; it tempts you to do things you can't take back.

The lie was thinking the secrets made them closer.

All evil begins with a curiosity of darkness.

It's beautiful, really, to watch how quickly one's heart can learn to love new people, new souls ... if ever one is brave enough to give it the opportunity.

When I close my eyes, I see a moonlit lagoon with nothing but the future reflecting over its concealed depths. When I open my eyes, I see you. The moon turns to sun, and a whole city arises from the waters—a city made of us, a city made of dreams.

Entering the room, I froze. I'm still unsure as to what drew my attention to them. But it was beautiful. He stood leaning against the wall, eyes fixed on hers, opposite the room. I was captivated—well, jealous mostly—of a connection so pure with another human. They were saying so much without speaking a word.

Her green eyes glistened as she returned to her chatting friends. He then folded into the crowd, chuckling to himself about the silent conversation they shared.

You can always tell a pair in love; they sparkle with that certain magic only love can bring.

Maybe that's what love is. When you no longer need to mean something to everyone. When seeing your name in lights for the purpose of being recognized is no longer important. Because you know you mean everything to that one person, and you realize that is – and will always be – enough.

The brave ones are my favorites.

I'm tired. Tired of my heart painfully and tirelessly searching for a place that once was, when all I really want is to find a new place, a new heart—and all it wants is to find home again in the company of you.

Do something today that lets someone know the world deserves them in it another day.

Let's get lost. Let's go to a place never to be seen again. But not a small town where our souls could get bored. Instead, let's hide among millions. Let's go to a place where our hearts will never sleep. Run away with me. Let's get lost in the city.

"Such an awful thing to see a child go so young," the lady gossiped. "What did you hear was the cause: failure of the heart?"

"We shouldn't speak of an ended life like the rest of the stories able to be replaced by something different tomorrow," retorted the nearby guest. "She took her own life, so I'd say failure of the soul."

"Look," said the old man, pointing to a butterfly gleaming in the summer sun. "She's the most beautiful thing I've ever seen."

"How do you know it's a she?" questioned the young boy.

"Because," replied the man, "her colors could make the most depressed souls thankful to be alive another day, but she's flown into the hollow of that tree."

"So?"

"It's easy," the old man continued. "She's a girl because she's perfect, but she's hiding."

You were different yet attractive because you were different ... so genuinely content in being alone. Like a star so powerfully magnificent by itself, you couldn't possibly hide it behind the title "constellation."

The scary thing is the more I look at our society, the more I realize it really is survival of the fittest. You don't have to be around long to realize the weakest are quickly overlooked. I think we all have discovered that love, in whatever form, is strength. So we're left hopelessly desperate for someone to love, hoping they'll grant us the strength we lack and dangerously unconcerned with who that someone is.

Passion is what drives you; hard work is what makes you; humility is what sets you apart.

Returning home without her was cold ... foreign. But the wood floors still echoed her footsteps, and the illuminated lampshades still seemed to tease the shadows of her hair. Returning home without her created the unavoidable realization of the crevice-filling laughter previously taken for granted.

Somebody once asked my definition of *forever*. I think forever can be defined similarly to love—both too extraordinary to be fully comprehended and defined. Like love, you can experience forever in a lifetime, and it's always experienced differently for everyone. But for us, laughing over cappuccinos in some bistro off Fifth Avenue is just another love-filled forever placed in the sequence of a lifetime.

There's nothing I love more than strolling through a spring-awakened boulevard with you.

The solid home that they built turned into a hollow house that he left.

I will never sacrifice my standards for you. And if this were really love, you would never ask me to.

My error was thinking you couldn't live without me. In doing so, I made you want to.

She hated him because he took away her innocent view of the world ... where love came easily and heartbreak was rare. After him, it wasn't really the loss of him that hurt, but the rude awakening to the real world.

It's only right to kiss a girl when she's fully in love with who she is. For kisses don't create love; they distract from the places without it.

If you're not ready to give second chances, you're not ready for love.

You're the show I sit through all the advertisements for.

She didn't believe anything, but with him, she saw everything. And by opening her eyes, he made her believe.

I want a lifetime of running into your arms as fast as my high heels will allow.

Here's the thing: you won't have them long.

I looked at the stars and thought, *How easy it is to get used to a miracle.*

Love is desire antagonizing fate.

Find your something.

They were in love, just two souls that crossed and found each other to be great company.

You're rare like gold, silver ... antique-car rare. The dark has seen enough of you; now it's time to show the light.

I have a strange longing to pen a thousand letters of emotions too raw to speak. So years from now, I'll venture into some musty cellar for the sole purpose of unfolding the dusty pages to finger the feelings I never allowed myself to embrace.

She was before her time. Placed in a generation too blind to love someone so unlike the standard they had made themselves.

She danced in her sandals with such unearthly bliss that even the coldest of hearts dared to smile.

The
DANCE

The child soon stumbled upon the controversial and problematic question: is growing up really worth it?

How long can we keep children pure? How long can we keep them contentedly themselves before the world tries to tell them otherwise?

Let them write their story.

She never stopped dreaming of the future, but when the future turned present, it wasn't hers. So she grew the courage to leave and make her own.

It's healthy to be spontaneous—to jump in a car and drive toward whatever makes you happiest.

The adventure of life is not knowing what'll come next. Maybe that's why tomorrows are so enticing.

What they choose to show you isn't always who they are.

If you ask me, imagination isn't something we grow but something we allow ourselves to expand.

I've come to realize that happy isn't really a state of being. And realizing that it didn't have to be left me free to embrace the passing moments that make me smile.

Empowerment was the feeling I received when I realized I deserved more than fair-weather friends.

I closed my eyes, thinking of all the people I could affect in a lifetime if I made a point to reach out. In the height of my lucid dream, a whole assembly of changed tomorrows arose. It was then I realized anyone with a purpose can change the future. Despite the divergence this can create, I'll take my chances. I hope you take yours.

Some days, I want to be cliché, to jump on a plane, fly to Paris, and like millions before, imagine my dreams in the shadow of the Eiffel Tower.

Why do we casually play with time, acting as though we're entitled to a tomorrow?

There's nothing vibrant in tomorrow for the one who's left behind.

She wasted so much time chasing their standard of beauty because no one told her she already was.

Some days, there's nothing colder than the blizzard of your thoughts.

What a world this would be if we all became beautifully receptive to, and genuinely unthreatened by, ideas that contradicted our own.

We don't search for a definition in art; we quietly let each piece uniquely speak to us. In the same way, I wonder what great things we'd learn from great humans if we just once hesitated to speak.

Despite good intentions, shelter from the truth only leaves one unprepared for the storm.

In the dark of the tunnel, please know this truth: the light is ahead, so just see this through. The world is in need of more strong souls like you.

In dangerous waters, we learn to navigate without view of the shore.

Time will disappear before you realize who stole it.

If you realized your full potential, what more would you be doing to reach it?

Unlike others, his perfection didn't fool her. Someone so visibly good at everything had to be covering an otherwise invisible something.

I do hope that in this technological age, we are never able to define the infinite. For definition makes the infinite finite, and anything finite loses its beauty.

You're human; you're worth it.
You're different; you're worth it.
You're tarnished; you're worth it.
You're you; you're priceless.

Hey there. Yeah, you. You're beautiful, you perfect, irreplaceable soul.

As you build your kingdom, remember who helped you lay the bricks.

I'm happy you're alive.

She wasn't passionate but loving.
She wasn't dangerous but strong.
She wasn't wild but free.

It's like you're a tree, a beautiful, blossoming, tree.
And every piece of yourself you choose to share
with me feeds the fire of my soul.

I don't think any of us will achieve our personal standard of perfection. So to spare a lifetime of disappointment, let's learn to love the imperfections.

It seemed unfair the world kept spinning when her world seemed to stop.

She stood paralyzed as she watched her greatest fear come to life—her dreams fading into the past, leaving nothing in her tomorrow to look forward to.

What if all you think you know is just an illusion of what you're afraid to discover?

Let's be a generation that brings the cautious out of the shadows instead of dusting them into the dark.

When did we define self-care as selfish?

"You want to know the secret?" the old millionaire whispered into the ear of her granddaughter from her deathbed. "They trick you," she hissed. "They tell you to live to change tomorrow, so I lie here, with death knocking at my door, grieving over the todays I've lost instead of celebrating the tomorrows I've changed."

Would the pioneers of the past look at your life and be thankful for their sacrifice?

The sun wasn't shown the details of its commitment to shine forever. The immediate destruction that would result should the sun leave its post is unimaginable. We know the sun will remain until forever finds an ending; that's commitment. So why do we excuse ourselves from the reality of commitment? When did we begin to accept the consequences and destruction of broken promises as collateral damage? When did we allow a promised forever to become temporary?

She always wore diamonds when there were others around to see them. She never knew she could attract genuine people if she showed them her heart of gold.

The key to finding what's forgotten is looking in the dusty places.

They ended their night with the humor of their shared folly, for they continually lived thinking they were above any unplanned tragedy, despite every contrary example that life doesn't hand out quotas. When you've had your share of heartache, betrayal, and disappointments, you take what you've been given each day and try to grow from there.

Who said the lines can't be redefined?

We're all running either toward or away from something, except life doesn't stop to make sure you can keep up. Your job is to make sure while you're still running, you're trying to help up whoever has fallen along the way.

It's natural to want to be remembered. But we should want to be remembered for the right reasons. I want to be remembered, even by just a few, as an example that feeling, loving, hurting, and living are worth it.

This world will kill a person if left to live it alone.

Sometimes the hardest thing of all is remembering our mortality.

Alone, winning was winning, and losing was losing. But with him, losing was unequivocal.

Life will continue to spiral if you don't try to stop the cycle.

He felt sorry for her blindly doing everything for everyone with no one expecting her to do otherwise. It was as though her whole life were a car, and she allowed herself to be chauffeured because she was too afraid to take the wheel herself.

The past won't stop haunting you until you stop protecting it.

My greatest puzzlement is that we so earnestly make plans for an unpromised tomorrow as if there's not enough greatness in today.

All I want are endless summers, unforgettable sunsets, ever-sparkling shores, and eternal life.

The nights were when he imagined a life other than his own. The days were when he created it.

I am struggling to cope with my sudden awakening to reality.

Pick your poison: the dangerous or the comfortable. Either way, they're both deadly.

Her dreams were as elusive as a wild fox ... never really something she could find but something that would eventually find her if she journeyed long enough.

The fact that I don't plan isn't because I'm unorganized; I just like to see what stories time writes all on her own.

I don't know if she would recognize me. "She" being the girl I was then. I've changed, I suppose, due to too many days acting in the theater of life, my insecurities selfishly casting the characters most unlike myself.

I used to lie awake at night creating stories in my head. But now, I fall asleep to the tales that have already taken place, because the story I'm living is finally grand enough.

I think all anybody asks of anyone else is genuine acceptance of who they are.

With love, we're all given the chance to live infinitely.

What are you afraid of? It always seems to be fear that's keeping us from going after what we want.

I love you to forever and back.

The bird's song at dusk in the summer gives me a strange longing to stay in this broken world forever.

I've found there is no better medicine for a tired heart than lying in the grass, not thinking of tomorrow, yesterday, or even the events of the current day. But to just be, looking at the darkening sky, waiting for the stars.

The world is your stage. Step out, and perform the dance of your heart.

Grace VanSciver

Printed in the United States
By Bookmasters